TABLE OF CONTENTS

WORKBOOK 2

LESSONS 1-7

AMERICAN ENGLISH

THE PRACTICAL WAY

WORK BOOK 2

JEAN PACHTER
IN COLLABORATION WITH
CAROL SWILL

AMERICAN LANGUAGE
COMMUNICATION CENTER

Published by
American Language Communication Center, Inc.
New York, N.Y. 10018

ISBN: - 10: 0-99-071965-0
13: 978-0-9907196-5-6

Printed in the United States of America

READING

A SUMMER VACATION

As you, know, Betty and Kathy want to go to the Vacation Time Hotel for their summer vacation. Susan wants to go there, too.

Miss Smith: Vacation Time Hotel.
Susan: Yes, please. I want to ***make a reservation*** for one week.
Miss Smith: All right. When do you plan to get here?
Susan: I plan to get there on July 17th.
Miss Smith: And when do you plan to leave?
Susan: I plan to leave on July 24th. Is there a lake near the hotel?
Miss Smith: Yes, there is. It is next to the picnic area. Can you swim?
Susan: Yes, I can swim very well.
Miss Smith: That's good.
Susan: And one more question please. How is the weather there in the summer?
Miss Smith: It is hot in the daytime, but it is not ***muggy***. The ***temperature*** is usually around 75°. And it is cool at night.
Susan: That sounds wonderful. I want to make a reservation.

SUBSTITUTION DRILLS

I plan to get there on July 17th.
August 20th
October 14th
May 9th
June 21st

Can you swim?
dance
run
play tennis
ride a horse

It is not muggy.
rainy
cloudy
cool
cold

The temperature is 75°.
62°
51°
40°
83°

Fill in with the correct word.

SWIM, WEATHER, MAKE A RESERVATION, NEXT TO, GET HERE, MUGGY, MORE

1. I want to___________ ____________ ____________for one week.
2. When do you plan to ____________ ____________?
3. The lake is ____________ ____________ the picnic area.
4. How is the ____________ there in the summer?
5. It is hot in the daytime, but it is not ____________.
6. Can you _____________?
7. One _____________ question, please.

QUESTIONS

1. When does Susan plan to get to the hotel?
2. When does she plan to leave?
3. Where is the lake?
4. Can Susan swim?
5. How is the weather in the summer?
6. Can you swim?

MY TELEPHONE NUMBER IS 643-2619.

1. Ask a question and answer it.

Example: 473-7960

WHAT IS YOUR TELEPHONE NUMBER?
MY TELEPHONE NUMBER IS FOUR SEVEN THREE-SEVEN NINE SIX OH.

624-7310 359-6528 336-4210

724-1639 787-1610

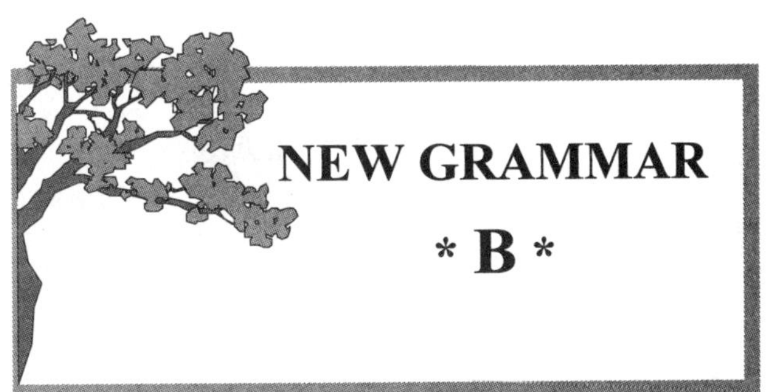

DO YOU HAVE SINGLES?

1. Ask a question and answer it.

Example: $5

A: EXCUSE ME, DO YOU HAVE CHANGE OF FIVE DOLLARS? I NEED SOME SINGLES.

B: SURE, HERE YOU ARE.
(NOTE: SOME = A FEW)

1. $10
2. $25
3. $15
4. $30
5. $50
6. $100

THE 4 SEASONS

1. **<u>Ask a question and answer it</u>.**

Example: **WINTER/BEGIN/WHEN**

WHEN DOES WINTER BEGIN?
WINTER BEGINS IN DECEMBER.

1. Spring/begin/when?
2. Spring/end/when?
3. Fall/end/when?
4. Winter/end/when?
5. Summer/begin/when?
6. Fall/begin/when?
7. Winter/begin/when?

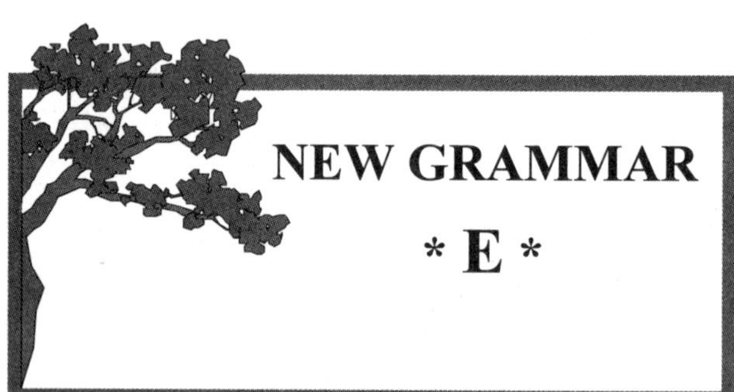

THE WEATHER

1. **Ask and answer the question. Use "is it" or "does it" in your question.**

Example: **SUNNY/WHEN? (SUMMER)**
WHEN IS IT SUNNY?
IT IS SUNNY IN SUMMER.

SNOW/WHEN? (WINTER)
WHEN DOES IT SNOW?
IT SNOWS IN WINTER.

1. Hot/when?/(summer)
2. Freezing/when/ (winter)
3. Rain/when?/(fall)
4. Muggy/when?/(summer)
5. Cool/when?/(fall)
6. Windy/when?/(fall)
7. Snow/when? /(winter)
8. Humid/when?/(summer)

NEW GRAMMAR

*** F ***

MARK LIVES ON THE 4TH FLOOR.

1. **Change from a regular number to an ordinal number. Don't forget to say "the".**

Example: **EIGHT (FLOOR)**
THE EIGHTH FLOOR.

1. Three (floor)
2. Ten (house)
3. Twelve (student)
4. Three (building)
5. Four (horse)
6. Twenty-five (woman)
7. Seventy-one (can)
8. Ninety-one (bottle of beer)
9. One (child)
10. Thirty-one (day)

THE 20TH
THE TWENTIETH

PRACTICE

1. Change to an ordinal number. Do not forget to say “the”.

Example: **60 (HOUSE)**
THE SIXTIETH HOUSE.

1. 20 (man)
2. 40 (suit)
3. 90 (envelope)
4. 50 (ping-pong ball)
5. 70 (souvenir)
6. 30 (payment)
7. 80 (road map)

CAN YOU DANCE?
YES, I CAN DANCE.

1. Change to a sentence with "can".

Example: **I WALK ONE HOUR EVERY DAY.**
I CAN WALK ONE HOUR EVERY DAY.

1. You play soccer very well.
2. I write letters in English.
3. I cook turkey on Thanksgiving.
4. I write interesting letters.
5. They paint the house.
6. They read the newspaper.
7. You fly an airplane.
8. You dance very well.
9. I speak English.
10. They save money.

THEY CAN SKATE.
THEY LIKE TO SKATE.

1. <u>Change to a sentence with "can".</u>

Example: **I LIKE TO PLANT FLOWERS.**
I CAN PLANT FLOWERS.

1. I want to build a house.
2. Susan likes to make scrambled eggs.
3. My grandmother likes to cook.
4. We want to ***<u>decorate</u>*** the house.
5. They like to go for a walk in the evening.
6. Sheila likes to cut my hair.
7. The puppies want to catch the ball.
8. I want to take a vacation.
9. We like to drive on the highway.
10. Sharon likes to cook dinner.
11. John wants to change the flat tire.
12. The teacher likes to explain the lesson.

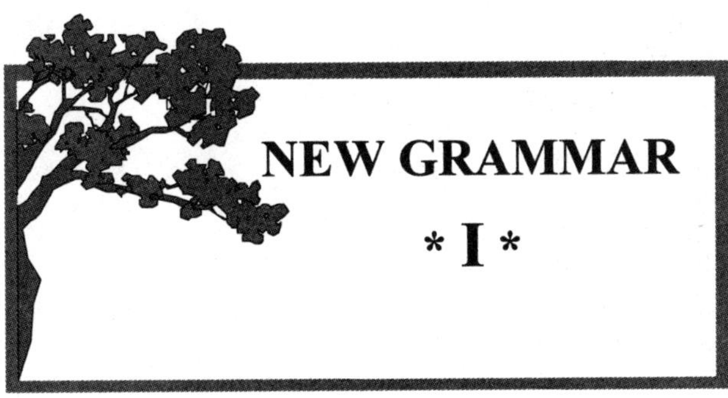

I CANNOT SPEAK RUSSIAN.

1. Answer the questions with "cannot".

Example: **CAN JOHN TYPE?**
NO, HE CANNOT TYPE.

1. Can we eat these vegetables?
2. Can Larry visit us next weekend?
3. Can John and Mary dance well together?
4. Can Patty get up early tomorrow?
5. Can Linda play the guitar?

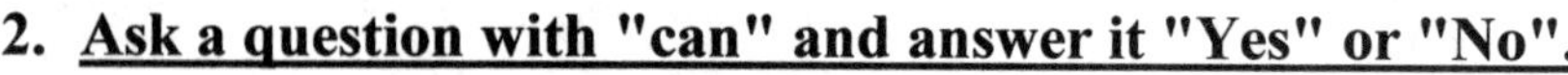

2. Ask a question with "can" and answer it "Yes" or "No".

Example: **FIX THE TYPEWRITER / SUSAN? (YES)**

CAN SUSAN FIX THE TYPEWRITER?
YES, SHE CAN FIX THE TYPEWRITER.

1. Type/Mary? (Yes)
2. Operate a computer/John? (No)
3. Answer the telephone /they? (Yes)
4. Cook/you? (Yes)
5. Write short letters/Kathy? (Yes)
6. Make strong coffee/they? (No)
7. Play baseball/the boys ? (No)
8. Take a vacation/the president? (Yes)
9. See in the dark/you? (No)
10. Climb a tree/Mr. Smith? (Yes)
11. Hang a picture/Mrs. Smith? (No)
12. Type fast/the secretary? (Yes)

3. Write the answers to these questions.

1. Can you swim?

____

2. Can you ski?

____

3. Can you play the piano?

____

4. Can you sing?

____

5. Can you dance?

____

6. Can you cook very well?

____

7. Can you paint?

____

ASK YOUR PARTNER THE ABOVE QUESTIONS.

IS THERE A RESTROOM ON THE FLOOR?

1. Change from a sentence to a question.

Example: **THERE IS A PLANT IN THE ROOM.**
IS THERE A PLANT IN THE ROOM?

1. There is a butcher shop on the corner.
2. There is a dry cleaner on this street.
3. There is a plate in the sink.
4. There is a guard at the bank.
5. There is a ticket office at the airport.
6. There is a roach in the kitchen.
7. There is a letter in the mailbox.
8. There is a stop sign at the corner.
9. There is a receptionist at the front desk.
10. There is a church in the town.

READING

TELEPHONE INFORMATION

As you know, Sally is at the park today.

After three hours, Sally leaves the park. She has to go to a party tonight, and she is a little late. She decides to make a call. There is a ***public telephone*** near the entrance of the park. Sally needs ***exact change***.

She doesn't remember her friend's phone number, so she calls ***information***. Sally is in Manhattan now, and her friend is in Brooklyn, so she dials 1 ***plus*** the area code (718) plus (555-1212). That call is free. After the operator gives Sally her friend's number, she calls her friend. She then goes to the bus stop.

She ***waits on line*** for the bus. Does she have the exact change? Sometimes simple things are very complicated.

SUBSTITUTION DRILLS

There is a public telephone near the entrance.
the elevator
the ladies' room
the door
the pizza place

She doesn't remember her friend's phone number.
lawyer's
doctor's
dentist's
teacher's

She waits on line at the bus stop.
subway station
post office
supermarket
bank

Fill in with the correct word.

LEAVES, EXACT CHANGE, INFORMATION, WAITS ON LINE, PUBLIC TELEPHONE, AREA CODE, COMPLICATED

1. There is a__________ __________ near the entrance.
2. Sally needs __________ __________ for the telephone.
3. She doesn't remember her friend's phone number, so she decides to call __________.
4. She dials 1 plus the__________ __________ (718).
5. She __________ __________ __________ for the bus.
6. After 3 hours Sally __________ the park.
7. Sometimes simple things are very __________.

QUESTIONS

1. Where does Sally have to go tonight?
2. Where is the public telephone?
3. What does she need?
4. What number does Sally dial?
5. Do you often call information?
6. Can you understand the telephone operator?
7. What does Sally need for the bus?
8. Do you usually take the bus or the subway?
9. Do you always have a token?
10. How many tokens do you usually buy?

THINK AND WRITE

Write 5 sentences about what you can do and two sentences about what you cannot do.

Example: **I CAN PLAY THE PIANO.**
I CANNOT SING.

1. ______________________________
2. ______________________________
3. ______________________________
4. ______________________________
5. ______________________________
6. ______________________________
7. ______________________________

QUIZ

Answer the questions.

1. How much money do you have today? (answer with dollars and cents)

____

2. Can you speak English well?

____

3. Do you like to clean your apartment?

____

4. Can you fly?

____

5. How is the weather today?

____

6. The temperature is 55°. Is it hot today?

____

7. There are beautiful flowers in the park. What season is it?

____

8. What floor do you live on?

____

9. Is there a teacher in your classroom?

____

10. Where is the teacher?

____

A NEW APARTMENT

Harold wants a new apartment. The landlord shows him an apartment.

Harold: Are there many closets in this apartment?

Landlord: Yes, there are five closets. And there is a ***terrace***. Only a few apartments have a terrace. And there is also an ***air-conditioner***.

Harold: I really like this apartment. I want to paint it blue. Is that OK? I can paint very well.

Landlord: Yes, that's OK. But don't paint it dark blue, please.

Harold: Sure.

Landlord: Let's go ***downstairs*** to my office. Can you give me a ***deposit*** of $100.00 today?

Harold: Sure. Here you go.

Landlord: Good. Now you have to ***sign*** this ***lease***. Read it carefully and sign ***on the bottom***. please.

SUBSTITUTION DRILLS

Are there many closets in this apartment?
lights
outlets
windows
radiators

Let's go downstairs to my office.
the lobby
the super
the manager
the basement

You have to sign this lease.
contract
check
letter
paper

Can you give me a deposit today?
now
right now
at this time
tomorrow

Fill in with the correct word.

LANDLORD, DEPOSIT, TERRACE, BOTTOM, DOWNSTAIRS, LEASE, PAINT

1. There are five closets. And there is also a ___________________.
2. Let's go ___________________ to my office.
3. Can you give me a ___________________ today, please?
4. You have to sign this ___________________.
5. Sign at the ___________________, please.
6. The ___________________ shows him an apartment.
7. I want to ___________________ it blue.

QUESTIONS

1. How many closets are there in the new apartment?
2. What color does Harold want to paint the new apartment?
3. What color is your apartment?
4. What does Harold give the landlord?
5. What does he have to sign?

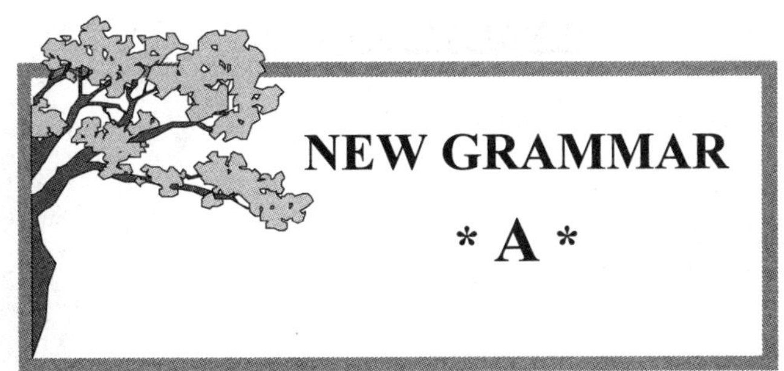

HOW MANY?

1. <u>Ask a question with "how many" and answer the question.</u>

Example: **PAGES/STUDY EVERY NIGHT/YOU (2)**

HOW MANY PAGES DO YOU STUDY EVERY NIGHT?
I STUDY 2 PAGES EVERY NIGHT.

1. Pages/read/every night/she (10)

2. Bananas/want in the morning/the monkey (4)

3 Hats/take to the beach/you (1)

4. Shirts/iron every Sunday/your mother (7)

5. Roses/buy/for her mother/Mary (8)

6. Cars/fix in a day/the mechanic (2)

ONE CHILD
TWO CHILDREN

PRACTICE

1. Make a question with "How many".

Example: **BOOK/READ/YOU?**
HOW MANY BOOKS DO YOU READ?

1. bottle/want/he?
2. American man/know/you?
3. class/take/you?
4. museum/want to visit/the tourist?
5. person/play soccer with/you?
6. battery/need/you?
7. child/have/they?
8. cake/want to bake/the cook?
9. phone call/get/the teenager?
10. student/have/the teacher?

2. Make another sentence with the correct plural form.

Example: **I HAVE ONE CHILD. MY FRIEND (2)**

MY FRIEND HAS TWO CHILDREN.

1. I know one woman in the office. My friend (4)
   My ____
2. I live with one person. My sister (2)
   My sister ____________________________________
3. The little girl has one new tooth. The little boy (4)
   The little boy _________________________________
4. The old man has one bad foot. The old woman (2)
   The old woman ________________________________
5. His room has one window. My room (2)
   My room ____________________________________
6. My skirt has one pocket. My jacket (2)
   My jacket ____________________________________
7. Sharon knows one man in her building. Susan (7)
   Susan ______________________________________

8. Debra likes one flower in the vase. Margaret (3)
   Margaret ____

9. Mary eats dinner with one man. John (4)
   John ____

10. My sister writes one letter at night. My brother (3)
   My brother ____

11. I can hear one child in the playground. He (16)
   He____

THERE ARE

1. Change these sentences to the plural.

Example: **THERE IS A MAN AT THE DOOR. (3)**
THERE ARE THREE MEN AT THE DOOR.

1. There is a puppy under the tree. (2)
2. There is a sharp knife in the drawer. (2)
3. There is a happy child in the playground. (5)
4. There is a chocolate chip cookie on the plate. (4)
5. There is a cigarette machine in the lobby. (2)
6. Look! There is a baseball player on the bus. (5)
7. There is a dentist on the fourth floor. (2)
8. There is a dictionary in the bookcase. (3)

2. <u>Change the sentence to the singular.</u>

Example: **THERE ARE TWO WHITE BLOUSES IN THE <u>WASHING MACHINE</u>.**
THERE IS A WHITE BLOUSE IN THE WASHING MACHINE.

1. There are two frogs in the lake.
2. Be careful! There are three snakes in the grass.
3. There are only 6 leaves on the tree.
4. There are two children on the swings.
5. There are five secretaries in the office.
6. There are three handsome men in the cafeteria.
7. There are four cups of hot chocolate on the tray.
8. There are two women on the bench.

CAN YOU.... MEANINGS #1 AND #2

1. <u>Make a question with "Can you". Say "Please" for meaning number 2.</u>

Example: **RUN FAST?**
CAN YOU RUN FAST?

OPEN THE WINDOW?
CAN YOU OPEN THE WINDOW, PLEASE.

1. Dance well?
2. Carry my suitcase?
3. Do this math problem?
4. Lift weights?
5. Remember the lesson?
6. Touch the ceiling?
7. Give me some money?
8. Take out the garbage?
9. Make the bed?

CLOSE THE WINDOW, PLEASE.

1. Change to a sentence with "Can you.....please?".

Example: **CLOSE THE WINDOW, PLEASE.**
CAN YOU CLOSE THE WINDOW, PLEASE?

1. Take a message, please.
2. Repeat the sentence, please.
3. Pay for the class on Monday, please.
4. Call me tonight, please.
5. Go to the store for me, please.
6. Fix the television, please.
7. Sew a button on my blouse, please.
8. Turn on the answering machine, please.

PLEASE, DON'T CLOSE THE DOOR.

1. <u>Change to a negative sentence with "Don't".</u>

Example: **GET ME A CUP OF TEA, PLEASE.**
PLEASE, DON'T GET ME A CUP OF TEA.

1. Bring me the slippers, please.
2. Eat raw fish at the party, please.
3. Go to the cafeteria on the third floor, please.
4. Stand on the corner and drink beer, please.
5. Stay in the house all day, please.
6. Put my expensive blouse in the washing machine, please.

MANY STUDENTS
A FEW STUDENTS

1. <u>Make another sentence with "only a few".</u>

Example: **I WATCH MANY TV PROGRAMS. (MY SISTER)**
MY SISTER WATCHES ONLY A FEW PROGRAMS.

1. My mother irons many shirts. (I)
2. My teacher speaks many languages. (my classmate)
3. The farmer has many animals. (I)
4. There are many birds in the trees. (on the ground)
5. The men read many newspapers. (the teenagers)
6. The children play many games. (the parents)
7. Americans eat many cheeseburgers. (French)

8. There are many books in the library. (in the doctor's office)

9. Teenagers have many pimples. (adults)

10. Bob works many hours. (Alan)

2. <u>Answer these questions.</u>

Example: **DOES THE CHILD HAVE MANY TOYS?** **(A FEW)**
NO, THE CHILD HAS A FEW TOYS.

DO YOU KNOW MANY PEOPLE? **(YES)**
YES, I KNOW MANY PEOPLE.

1. Are there many trees in the park? (a few)

2. Are there many plates on the table? (yes)

3. Are there many dresses in the closet? (yes)

4. Do they have many cassettes? (a few)

5. Does the cat have many kittens? (yes)

6. Does the fisherman catch many fish? (a few)

7. Does the rock star have many fans? (yes)

8. Are there many empty chairs in the classroom? (a few)

9. Are there many cans in the cupboard? (no)

10. Does the secretary type many letters or only a few letters? (a few)

DIALOGUE

NEW YEAR'S EVE IN NEW YORK

It is 11:00 p.m. There is a New Year's Eve party at Sandra's house. John and Allan are at the door now.

Sandra: Hi! Happy New Year, John. Mary is here ***already***.
John: Oh, good. Sandra, this is my ***best friend*** Allan from Nebraska.
Sandra: Nebraska? OK! How do you like New York, Allan?
Allan: It is ***fantastic***. There are so many interesting places here.
Sandra: Give me your coats, please. Do you want a drink now?
John: Can you give me a scotch and soda, please?
Sandra: Sure. And you, Allan?
Allan: I want a glass of white wine.
Mary: Hi, John. Happy New Year.
John: Mary, this is my best friend Allan from Nebraska.
Mary: Hi, Allan. Can you dance?
Allan: Sure. Let's dance.

HAPPY NEW YEAR!!!

PRACTICE

SUBSTITUTION DRILLS

Can you give me a scotch and soda, please?
beer
cup of coffee
coke
glass of wine

Can you do the tango?
merenge
cha-cha-cha
twist
bossanova

Fill in with the right word.

COATS, NEW YEAR'S EVE, BEST, ALREADY, WINE, AT, INTERESTING

1. There is a ________________ _________________ Eve party at Sandra's house.
2. This is my ________________ friend Allan from Nebraska.
3. Mary is here ________________.
4. I want a glass of white ________________.
5. John and Allan are ________________ the door.
6. There are so many ________________ places here.
7. Give me your ________________, please.

QUESTIONS

1. What day is it?
2. What does Allan want to drink?
3. What does John want to drink?
4. What do you drink on New Year's Eve?
5. Do you go to a party on New Year's Eve?
6. Can you dance?
7. Do you like to go to parties?
8. Where is your best friend?
9. Do you talk to him/her every day?
10. What does your best friend do?

READING

HAPPY BIRTHDAY TO YOU

Only a few adults have birthday parties. Usually, adults get many cards for their birthday. The cards are from friends, ***co-workers*** and ***relatives***. Sometimes, adults have a birthday dinner with friends. They have a birthday cake and wine, too.

Some adults don't like to ***celebrate*** their birthday.

Some adults have a big party. They dance and talk a lot. They meet many old friends. Many parties in the U.S. are casual. Young people usually wear ***jeans***. After the party, the ***host or hostess*** ***cleans up***. A birthday party is hard work, but it is a lot of fun!

Happy birthday to you, young or old!

SUBSTITUTION DRILLS

Only a few adults have birthday parties.

like men
go to
love
remember

Some adults don't like to celebrate their birthday.

women
children
people

Fill in with the correct word.

CO-WORKERS, HOST/HOSTESS, BIRTHDAY PARTY, TALK, YOUNG, CASUAL, CELEBRATE

1. The cards are from friends, ________________ and relatives.
2. Sometimes adults have a _____________ _____________with friends.
3. Some adults don't like to ________________ their birthday.
4. Parties in the US are usually ________________.
5. After the party the ________________ or ________________ cleans up.
6. They dance and ________________ a lot.
7. ________________ people usually wear jeans.

QUESTIONS

1. Do many adults have birthday parties?
2. Do adults get only a few cards?
3. Do adults have a birthday cake?
4. Who cleans up?
5. Do you get many cards on your birthday?
6. Do you like American cake?
7. What do young people usually wear to a party?
8. Are birthday parties fun?
9. Can you make a cake?
10. Do you like to wear casual clothes?

WRITE

Write a story about your apartment.

Example:

1. I have a beautiful apartment.
2. I live on the l0th floor. The walls are white.
3. There are three rooms in my apartment - a kitchen, a bedroom, and a living room.
4. There are three windows in my apartment.
5. I have a light blue carpet. It is expensive, but it is beautiful.

6 I have a white sofa and a brown desk.

Now, you write:

1. ____
2. ____
3. ____
4. ____
5. ____
6. ____

QUIZ

Make a question.

Example: LIKE TO DANCE/YOU
DO YOU LIKE TO DANCE?

1. Windows/in your apartment/how many

2. Oranges/eat/the children/how many

3. Students/happy

4. Climb a tree/the boys/can

5. Turn off the TV,please/you/can

6. Languages/speak/you/can/how many

7. Athlete/fast

8. Give me a glass of wine, please/you/can/

9. Many lights on the Christmas tree/there are

10. Go to New Year's Eve parties you/like

11. Sing well/you/can

12. Books/you have/how many

13. Sunny/today

THANKSGIVING DINNER

As you know, Carmen plans to go to Mary's house for Thanksgiving dinner.

Carmen: What time do you eat dinner?
Mary: Well, we eat dinner at 3:00, but you can come over before. We can listen to my new CD's and watch TV.
Carmen: Do I have to put on a dress?
Mary: You don't have to, but people usually ***dress up*** for Thanksgiving.
Carmen. Well I never wear a dress. Usually, I wear jeans with a jacket. Is that OK?
Mary: Yes, that's fine.

Fill in with the correct words.

USUALLY, COME OVER, DRESS UP, CD'S, PUT ON, JEANS, NEVER

1. We eat dinner at 3:00, but you can ____________ ____________ before.
2. Do I have to ____________ ____________ a dress?
3. Usually, I wear ____________.
4. People usually ____________ ____________ for Thanksgiving.
5. We can listen to my new ____________.
6. I ____________ wear a dress.
7. People ____________ dress up for Thanksgiving.

QUESTIONS

1. What time does Mary eat dinner?
2. When can Carmen come over?
3. What can they do when Carmen comes over?
4. Does Carmen have to wear a dress?
5. Does she usually wear a dress?
6. What does Carmen plan to wear?
7. What do you like to wear on a big holiday?

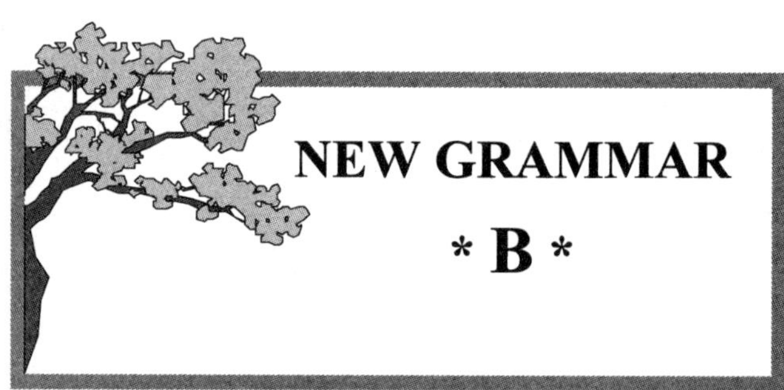

TURN ON - TURN OFF - GET UP -GET ON - GET OFF

JOYCE

Hi everybody. I am Joyce. I am a secretary, but I don't work for a company. I work in a doctor's office. I work very hard. I get _____________ the train at 8:00. I start work at 9:15.

I type letters, answer the phone, ***greet*** many people, and take care of the money. After work, I go home. I turn _____________ the TV and I watch the news. Then I feel ***relaxed.*** I don't eat dinner because it is usually too late. So I have a ***snack***. Then I read. After I read, I turn _____________ the light and I go to sleep.

Good night.

NEVER, SOMETIMES, USUALLY, OFTEN, ALWAYS

1. Change these sentences. Use the word in parentheses.

Example: MARY COOKS SPAGHETTI. (NEVER)
MARY NEVER COOKS SPAGHETTI.

1. Americans change their apartments. (often)

2. The teacher wears a suit. (always)

3. The teacher speaks slowly. (usually)

4. They play ball on Sunday. (often)

5. It rains in Arizona. (sometimes)

6. The people in my building have parties. (never)

7. My father gives me presents. (often)

8. My friend understands me. (always)

9. Children need a lot of milk. (usually)

10. That man drinks black coffee. (often)

11. We do the laundry on Monday. (always)

12. The students speak Spanish in class. (never)

I HAVE TO LEAVE NOW.

1. <u>Change to a sentence with "have to".</u>

Example: **MY PARENTS FLY TO AMERICA.**
MY PARENTS HAVE TO FLY TO AMERICA.

1. My friends carry my suitcase.

2. We go to the dentist.

3. We don’t go to the laundromat.

4. Mr. and Mrs. Smith call the plumber.

5. The doctors help the patients.

6. The guests don't sweep the floor.

7. They don’t get up early.

8. We don't answer the telephone.

9. The horses run around the track.

10. The maids clean the room.

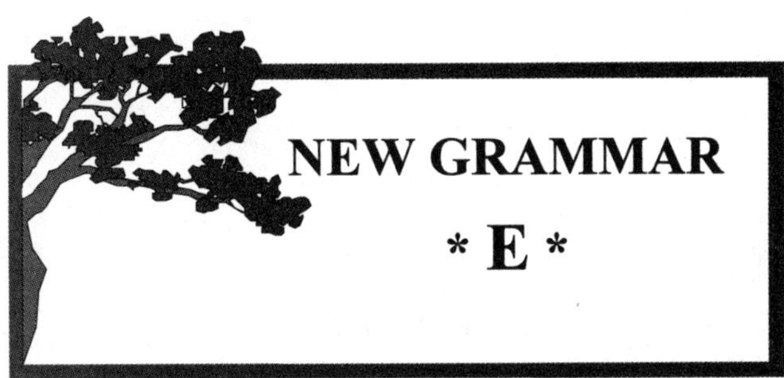

SHE HAS TO MAKE THE BED.

1. <u>Answer the question.</u>

Example: **WHEN DOES JOHN HAVE TO WASH THE FLOOR? (ON SATURDAY)**

HE HAS TO WASH THE FLOOR ON SATURDAY.

1. Where does he have to go every day? (to work)

2. Does Michael have to get a passport? (yes)

3. Does the cashier have to give change? (yes)

4. When does she have to put on a scarf? (in the winter)

5. What time does Sandra have to leave the party? (1:00 a.m.)

6. When does Betty have to buy a turkey? (on Thanksgiving)

DO THEY HAVE TO WALK THE DOG?

1. <u>Change to a question with "do" or "does".</u>

Example: **MARY HAS TO COOK. (LUNCH)**
DOES SHE HAVE TO COOK LUNCH?

1. The students have to understand the sentences. (the stories)
____?

2. The mailman has to deliver the letters. (the packages)
____?

3. We have to feed the cat. (the bird)
____?

4. My aunt has to bring the wine. (the cookies)
____?

5. Jane has to wash her hair. (her face)
____?

6. We have to buy new curtains. (blankets)

____?

7. Lisa has to make a cake. (cookies)

____?

8. The secretaries have to answer the phone. (the door)

____?

9. The women have to go to Macy's. (Walmart))

____?

10. The super has to clean the hallway. (stairs)

____?

WE DON'T HAVE TO LEAVE NOW.

1. <u>Change to a sentence with "don't" or "doesn't".</u>

Example: RITA HAS TO BUY WINE. (CHAMPAGNE)
SHE DOESN'T HAVE TO BUY CHAMPAGNE.

1. Michael has to drive a bus. (a truck)
2. They have to wash the dishes. (the pots)
3. I have to check my mailbox. (answering machine)
4. Martha has to wait for her husband. (her niece)
5 The boss has to pay the workers. (the customers)
6. The taxi drivers have to know the city. (the subway)
7. The rock star has to sing songs. (make jokes)

8. The farmers have to milk the cows. (feed the chickens)

9. The pharmacist has to prepare medicine. (food)

10. I have to talk to you. (her)

WHAT IS TODAY'S DATE?

1. <u>Ask the question and answer it.</u>

Example: **1749 (YEAR?)**

WHAT YEAR IS THIS?
THIS IS SEVENTEEN-FORTY-NINE.

1. 1989 (year?)
2. 1904 (year?)
3. 1960 (year?)
4. 2001(year?)
5. 1846 (year?)
6. 1553 (year?)

<u>ON</u> TUESDAY
<u>IN</u> APRIL
<u>IN</u> 1978
<u>IN</u> THE FALL

1. **Fill in with "in, on, at".**

Leroy is a policeman. Leroy usually works ______________ Fifth Avenue, but sometimes he works _________ Sixth Avenue. Leroy gets up early, puts on his ***uniform*** and leaves his house ______________ 7:00 in the morning. He gets ______________ his car and drives to work. Leroy carries a ***nightstick*** ______________ his hand. Today, there is a problem ______________ the playground. The little children are ______________ the playground. There are some mothers ______________ the benches. They have to take care of their babies.

But there is a problem. Three bad teenage boys are ______________ the entrance. Everybody knows these boys. They usually make trouble. When the boys see the policeman, they ***run away***. Leroy is happy. There is always a problem ______________ the playground ________________ the summer.

READING

CHUNG'S JOB

As you know, Chung is a nurse in a large hospital.

Chung is a very good nurse. She gets to work ***on time*** every day. She has to do many things every day. First she has to ***take*** a patient's ***temperature*** and she has to ***give shots***. She also ***changes the sheets*** every day. Chung wears comfortable white shoes, but at the end of the day her ***feet*** hurt a lot because she never sits down. At the end of the day she is tired, but she is very happy about her ***profession***.

SUBSTITUTION DRILLS

She gets to work on time every day.
to the office
to the hospital
to the factory

Chung wears comfortable white shoes.
big
old
new
expensive

She has to give shots..
change the sheets
bring the food
help the patients
take his temperature

She never sits down.
drinks coffee
shouts
cries
leaves work early

Fill in with the correct word.

**TEMPERATURE, NURSE, SHEETS,
ON TIME, PROFESSION, FEET, COMFORTABLE**

1. Chung is a very good ____________________.
2. She gets to work _____________ _____________ every day.
3. First, she has to take a patient's ____________________.
4. She also changes the ____________________ every day.
5. At the end of the day, her ____________________ hurt.
6. She is very happy about her ____________________.
7. Chung wears _________________ white shoes.

QUESTIONS

1. What does Chung have to do at work?
2. Can you take your temperature?
3. Can you give shots?

4. What kind of shoes does Chung wear?

5. Does she sit down at work or does she stand up?

6. Is Chung sad about her profession?

7. Do you want to be a nurse?

8. What do you want to be?

9. Do you change the sheets every day?

10. Do you make your bed every day?

REVIEW

THINK AND WRITE

Every Thanksgiving, Mary has a big party. She ***sends invitations*** to her friends. Here is Mary's invitation. Can you read it, please?

Dear John:

It is time to celebrate Thanksgiving.

Do you want to eat delicious turkey?

Do you want to drink wine?

Do you like to sing and dance? Of course you do!

Come to my party at 1290 1st Avenue.

Dinner is at 3:00, but you can come over at 2:00.

Please call me at (212) 777-1234 to give me your answer.

Mary

THANKSGIVING

Dinner Invitation

Now, you send an invitation to your friend.
Here is the invitation. Copy and complete it.

Dear ____________________:

It is time to ___________________________________.

Do you want to ____________________ at my house?

Do you like to ____________________?

Of course you do. Come to my party at:

(your address)

Dinner is at ____________________ but you can come over at ____________________.

Please call me at ____________________ and give me your answer.

QUIZ

ANSWER THE QUESTIONS.

1. Do you have to watch TV every night?
2. Do you have to pay for your English class?
3. Is your grandmother in New York?
4. What time do you get up?
5. Can you paint beautiful pictures?
6. Do you like to eat out ?
7. What do you have to do tonight?
8. Does your father have to work very hard?
9. Does your mother have to feed you?
10. Do you live far from the bus stop?

NEW GRAMMAR

* A *

WHERE ARE YOU GOING?
I AM GOING TO SCHOOL.

1. <u>Ask a question and answer it "Yes or No".</u>

Example: COOK/RICE ? NO

ARE YOU COOKING RICE?
NO, I AM NOT COOKING RICE.

1. Sleep/in class? ____?
   No ____

2. Walk/in the city? ____?
   No/in the country ____

3. Comb/your hair? ____?
   No/the dog's hair ____

4. ***<u>Sweep</u>***/the floor? ____?
   Yes ____

5. Call/your mother? ______________________________?
   No/friend ______________________________

6. Open the refrigerator? ______________________________?
   No/***cupboard*** ______________________________

7. Fold/the blouse? ______________________________?
   No/towel ______________________________

8. Plant/flowers? ______________________________?
   Yes ______________________________

9. Jog/in the street? ______________________________?
   No/in the park ______________________________

10. Feed/the cat? ______________________________?
    No/the baby ______________________________

11. Wait for/the bus? ______________________________?
    No/taxi ______________________________

12. Wear/sneakers? ______________________________?
    No/***high heels*** ______________________________

13. Relax/in the living room? ______________________________?
    No/in the backyard ______________________________

14. Sew/a dress? ______________________________?
    Yes ______________________________

2. Change the sentences to "ing". Use "now".

Example: I JOG EVERY MORNING.
I AM JOGGING NOW.

1. I relax every evening.

____

2. I play soccer on the weekend.

____

3. I put on ***perfume*** every morning.

____

4. I ***take off*** my shirt every evening.

____

5. I ***take out*** the garbage after dinner.

____

6. I ***snore*** every night.

____

7. I smoke in the afternoon.

____

8. I take a nap on ***rainy*** days.

____

9. I go shopping on Saturday.

____

10. I do the laundry in the morning.

____

11. I think about my country every day.

____

12. I ***polish*** my shoes every week.

____

3. Change to a sentence without "ing".

Example: **I AM CLEANING MY APARTMENT. (EVERY WEEK)**
I CLEAN MY APARTMENT EVERY WEEK.

1. I am painting a picture. (every Wednesday)

____

2. I am ***peeling potatoes***. (every evening)

____

3. I am setting the table. (before dinner)

____

4. I am putting on ***suntan lotion***. (in the summer)

____

5. I am watering the plants. (every day)

____

6. I am reading a sports magazine. (on Sunday)

____

7. I am opening presents. (on my birthday)

____

8. I am paying my bills. (every month)

____

9. I am typing a letter. (in the morning)

____

10. I am going swimming. (every summer)

____

11. I am listening to the teacher. (every day)

____

12. I am wearing a sweater. (every winter)

____

Can you help me with a story, please? Fill in the missing words.

Hello, everybody!

My name is Martha. I __________ from France. I __________ a tourist in New York. I __________ very busy. I__________ in school right now. I am__________ (listen) to the teacher right now. I __________ (listen) to the teacher ***every day***. I am also__________ (read) my English book now and I am __________ (write) the words in my notebook. I am also__________ (drink) coffee right now. I don't __________ (drink) coffee every day because it is very strong, but I am__________ (drink) coffee now.

QUESTIONS

1. Are you a tourist?
2. Are you busy?
3. Are you answering questions right now?
4. Are you writing in your notebook?
5. Are you listening to the teacher?

WHAT IS HE DOING?

1. Ask a question with "doing" and answer it.

Example: **HE?/COOKING DINNER.**

WHAT IS HE DOING?
HE IS COOKING DINNER.

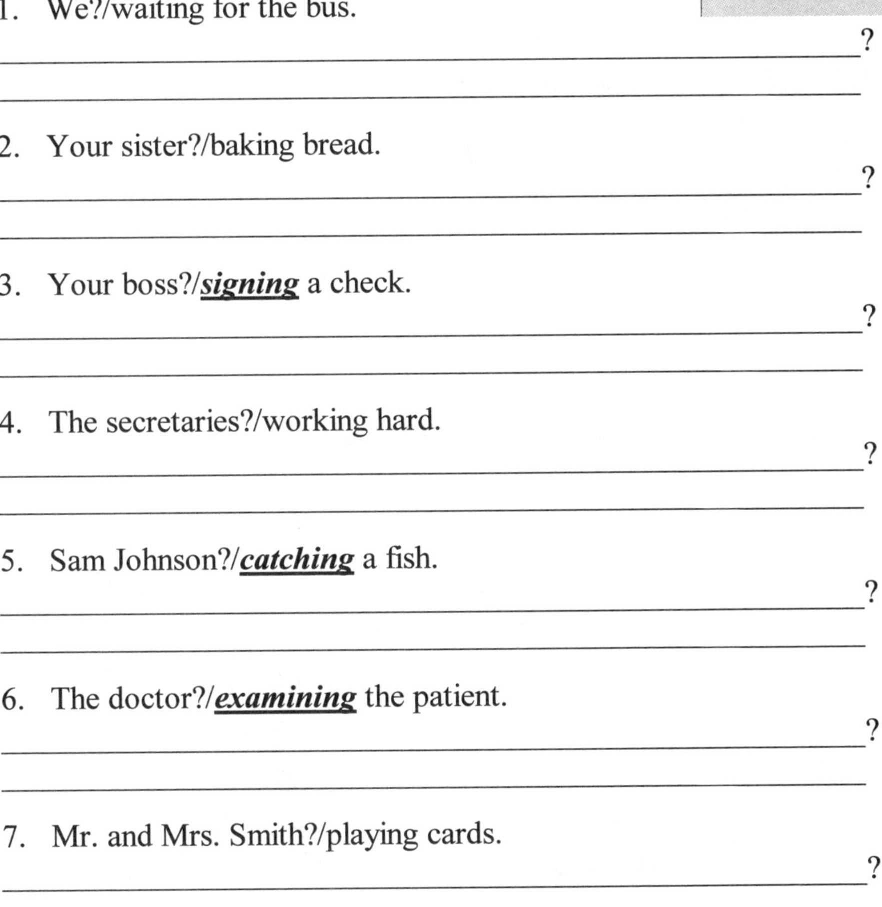

1. We?/waiting for the bus.

____?

____

2. Your sister?/baking bread.

____?

____

3. Your boss?/***signing*** a check.

____?

____

4. The secretaries?/working hard.

____?

____

5. Sam Johnson?/***catching*** a fish.

____?

____

6. The doctor?/***examining*** the patient.

____?

____

7. Mr. and Mrs. Smith?/playing cards.

____?

____

8. The people?/standing on line.

____?

____

9. The man?/pouring the wine.

____?

____

10. The customers?/buying clothes.

____?

____

11. The mechanics?/repairing the ***washing machine***.

____?

____

12. Janet Simpson?/carrying a package.

____?

____

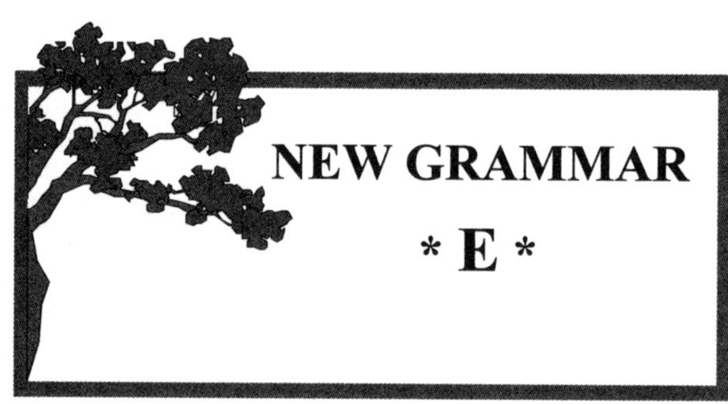

THERE ARE A LOT OF STUDENTS IN MY CLASS.
THERE ARE MANY STUDENTS IN HER CLASS.

1. <u>Change to a sentence with "many".</u>

Example: THERE ARE A LOT OF BOOKS ON THE SHELF. (ON THE TABLE, TOO)
THERE ARE MANY BOOKS ON THE TABLE, TOO.

1. There are a lot of oranges in the refrigerator. (in the basket, too)

____

2. There are a lot of ties in his drawer. (in his closet, also)

____

3. There are a lot of cars in the garage. (in the parking lot, too)

____

4. There are a lot of chairs on the lawn. (in the backyard, also)

____

5. There are a lot of presents under the tree. (on the table, too)

____

6. There are a lot of people in the coffee shop. (in the café, too)

____

2. <u>Change to a sentence with "many" or "a lot of".</u>

Example: THERE ARE ONLY A FEW JACKETS IN THE SMALL STORE. (MANY/IN/LARGE STORE)
THERE ARE MANY JACKETS IN THE LARGE STORE.

1. There are only a few pens on the desk. (many/in/drawer)

____

2. There are only a few bottles of beer on the table. (a lot of/in/refrigerator)

____

3. There are only a few handsome guys at this party. (many/in/disco)

____

4. There are only a few tomatoes on the plate. (a lot of/in/salad)

____

5. There are only a few newspapers in the supermarket. (many/at/newsstand)

____

6. There are only a few ***relatives*** at the Thanksgiving dinner. (many/at/wedding)

____

7. There are only a few paper clips on the desk. (a lot of/in/bag)

____

MONDAY MORNING

It is Monday morning. As you know, Rita, Rodney and Paula are going to work. It is now 8:00 AM. Rodney and Rita are walking ***down the block***. Rita is wearing a pink sweater. Rodney is wearing a blue suit. The ***coffee shop*** is open, but only a few people are ***inside***. Rodney is walking next to Rita, but he is not looking at her or talking to her. He is looking at the ***ground*** and he is ***frowning***. He is frowning because he is thinking about his boss. He doesn't like his boss. Rodney's boss shouts at him almost every day, and he always ***complains about*** Rodney's work. Rodney wants to ***quit*** his job, but he has to look for another job first. Rita is ***smiling*** because she enjoys her job very much. Her boss is friendly. Rita is very ***lucky***.

The bus is on the corner. A lot of people are getting on the bus and a few people are getting off the bus. The bus is usually crowded during ***rush hour***. Rodney and Rita are not getting on the bus right now. They are ***kissing*** good-bye, because they are ***in love***.

SUBSTITUTION DRILLS

Rita is wearing a pink sweater.
purple sweater
blue jacket
red hat
yellow skirt

The coffee shop is open, but only a few people are ***inside***.
drugstore
laundromat
post office
barber shop

He is frowning because he is thinking about his boss.
landlord
manager
doctor
lawyer

He complains about Rodney's work.
apartment
friends
schedule
clothes

Rodney is walking next to Rita.
sitting
standing
running
lying

Fill in with the correct word.

FROWNING, IN LOVE, BLUE, SWEATER, COMPLAINS ABOUT, INSIDE, QUIT, RUSH HOUR, LUCKY, KISSING

1. Rita is wearing a pink ___sweater___.
2. Rodney is wearing a ___blue___ suit.
3. The coffee shop is open, but only a few people are ___inside___.
4. He is looking at the ground and he is ___frowning___.
5. Rodney's boss shouts at him and he always ___complais about___ Rodney's work.
6. Rodney wants to ___quit___ his job.
7. Rita is very ___lucky___.
8. The bus is usually crowded during ___rush___ ___hour___.
9. They are ___kissing___ good-bye.
10. They are ___in love___ ________.

QUESTIONS

1. It is 8:00 am. Where are Rodney and Rita walking?
2. What is Rita wearing?
3. What is Rodney wearing?
4. What is your classmate wearing?
5. Is Rodney looking at Rita?
6. Is he talking to Rita?
7. What is he looking at?
8. Is he smiling?
9. What is he doing? Why?
10. Is Rita frowning?
11. Does Rita hate her boss?
12. Are a few people getting on the bus?
13. How many people are getting on the bus?
14. How many people are getting off the bus?
15. Are Rodney and Rita getting on the bus?
16. What are they doing?

PROGRESSIVE SUBSTITUTION DRILLS

She is looking at the pretty trees.

flowers ______________________________
he ______________________________
they ______________________________
picking up ______________________________
dead ______________________________

Rita is getting ready for work.

school ______________________________
going to ______________________________
the Students ______________________________
the library ______________________________
the librarian ______________________________

A FRIENDLY TELEPHONE CONVERSATION

Alice is home now. She is talking to Robert on the phone. As you know, Alice wants to leave New York.

Robert: I'm glad you are not leaving, Alice. Are you happy?
Alice: I don't know, Robert. I am still miserable.
Robert: Why?
Alice: Well, everyone has a busy schedule. No one has time to talk or go for coffee.
Robert: What about the other students in your English class?
Alice: They're OK. But they are busy, too.
Robert: Listen, I can meet you in an hour at the coffee shop. Is that good?
Alice: Yes. We can talk more then. See you later.

1. Fill in with the correct word.

1. Alice ____talking____ to Robert now.
   (talk)
2. She ____is____ still miserable.
   (be)
3. Alice ____wants____ to leave New York.
   (want)
4. Can you ____meet____ me in an hour?
   (meet)
5. Nobody ____has____ time to go for coffee.
   (have)
6. Nobody ever ____talks____ to me.
   (talk)
7. I have to ____talk____ with my friend.
   (talk)

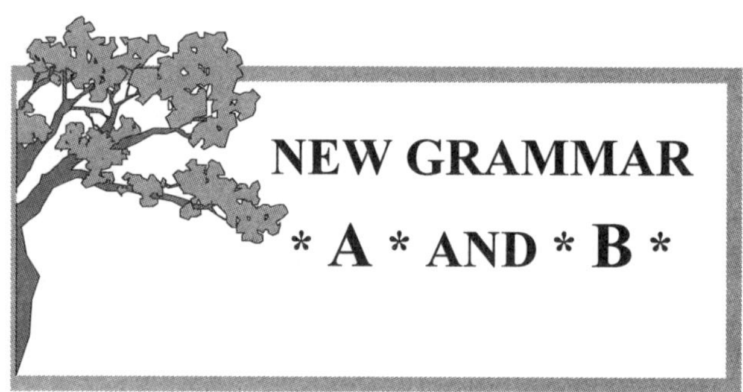

I DON'T WANT THIS BOOK.
GIVE ME ANOTHER BOOK, PLEASE.

PLEASE HELP ME WITH MY STORY.

1. Fill in with "another" or "the other".

IT IS 7:30

Tom and Jerry are going to the movies. Tom wants to see "Gone with the Wind" because he likes ***historical films***. Jerry doesn't want to see that movie; he wants to see ____another____ movie.

Now it is 8:00. Tom and Jerry are at the Blane Street twin theater (twin means two - there are two movies in the same theater). One movie is ***April the 15th*** Jerry doesn't want to see that movie. He wants to see ____the other____ movie in that theater. Before they sit down, they stop at the ***candy counter***. Tom buys a ***diet soda***. Jerry ***hates*** diet soda, so he wants ____the other____ soda. There is only one other kind of soda-orange/pineapple/banana ***combination***. Jerry still doesn't want a diet soda, so he buys ____another____ soda. He doesn't like it, but there is ***no other choice***.

DOES SHE TEACH ENGLISH?
IS SHE TEACHING ENGLISH?

1. <u>Use the simple form or the "ing" form.</u>

Remember: **Use the "ing" form only when you see or hear "am", "is", "are".**

Example:

DOES HE _________ WELL?	**(SPEAK)**	**DOES HE SPEAK WELL?**
IS HE _____________ ?	**(EAT)**	**IS HE EATING?**
SHE DOESN'T ________ HERE.	**(WORK)**	**SHE DOESN'T WORK HERE.**
THEY ARE NOT ___________.	**(WAIT)**	**THEY ARE NOT WAITING.**

1. Amy is not __sitting__ on the blanket right now. (sit)
2. The women are not __doing__ the laundry. (do)
3. My husband and I __talking__ a lot. (talk)
4. Where are you __working__ now? (work)
5. What time does he __arrive__ at work? (arrive)
6. Mary is not __leaving__ school now. (leave)
7. Mr. and Mrs. Collins __going__ on vacation every summer. (go)
8. What is he __cuting__ out of the magazine? (cut)
9. The dentist is not __cleaning__ my teeth right now. (clean)
10. The gardener __mow__ the lawn every spring. (mow)

2. <u>Make a sentence. Look at the time expression and use the simple form or the "ing" form.</u>

Example: **WORK OVERTIME/HE/SOMETIMES**
SOMETIMES, HE WORKS OVERTIME.

CLEAN MY DESK/I/NOW
I AM CLEANING MY DESK NOW.

1. Where/go/you/on Saturday?

___

2. What/cook/she/right now?

___

3. Not/drive to New York/Allan/right now.

___

4. Go away for the weekend/Judy/usually?

___

5. The men/build a house/now/where?

___

6. Take the subway/not/I/at night.

___

7. Call the doctor/you/now?

___

8. Fly/over the house/not/the airplane/right now.

___

9. He/put ketchup on his hamburger/not/usually.

___

10. The mechanic/fix the radiator/not/on Sunday.

___

AROUND IN A CIRCLE

Paula, Rodney and Rita are at Coney Island. They are eating cotton candy right now.

Paula: I love this cotton candy. And I love Coney Island. What's over there?
Rita: The rides. Do you want to go on the roller-coaster, Paula?
Paula: I am afraid of the roller-coaster. Can we go on another ride, please?
Rita: What are those people doing over there?
Rodney: They are ***waiting on line*** for the ***Rock and Roll Express***.
Rita: Is that a new ride?
Rodney: Yeah, it's new. You go around in a circle and you listen to rock music.
Rita: Oh, Rodney, you listen to rock music every day.
Rodney: Come on! It's a good ride! Let's try it!

They are now on the Rock and Roll Express.

Paula: Rodney!! I am getting ***dizzy***. Don't push ***against*** me.
Rodney: I can't stop.
Rita: Rodney! I am ***falling*** off this ride.
Rodney: You are not falling off the ride. ***Take it easy***.
Paula: I don't like this.
Rita: Are you ***holding on*** very ***tight***?
Paula: Of course I am.
Attendant: OK, all you wild ***rockers***. That's it! Do you want to go around ***another*** time?
Paula, Rita and Rodney: No Way!

SUBSTITUTION DRILLS

They are waiting on line for the Rock and Roll Express.
the ride
the roller-coaster
the cotton candy
the milkshakes

I'm getting ***dizzy***.
nervous
upset
worried
hungry

QUESTIONS

1. How does Paula feel on the Rock and Roll Express? She feels dizzy.
2. Is she holding on very tight? Yes, She is on very tight
3. Do they want go on another time? ~~Yes, they want go on another time~~
4. What is you favorite ride? My favorite ride is the roller-coaster
5. Is there a "Coney Island" in your country? No, there isn't in my...
6. When do you usually go there?
7. What do you do there?
8. Do you want to go to Coney Island? Yes, I want to go to Coney Island

Peter and Paul are at Coney Island. Peter likes everything, but Paul doesn't like anything. Look at their conversation.

Example: GO/RIDE/TOO DANGEROUS

PETER: LET'S GO ON THIS RIDE.

PAUL: I DON'T LIKE THIS RIDE. LET'S GO ON ANOTHER RIDE.

PETER: WHY DON'T YOU LIKE THIS RIDE?

PAUL: IT IS TOO DANGEROUS.

NOW YOU MAKE THE SAME CONVERSATION.

Let's Let's play this game.

I don't like I don't like this game.

Let's go on Let's play another game.

Why don't you Why don't you like this game?

It is too It is too boring.

1. eat/restaurant/too expensive
2. play/game/too boring
3. sit/bench/too uncomfortable
4. lie/blanket/too small
5. eat/ice-cream/too fattening
6. take/train/too crowded
7. use/beach umbrella/too light
8. drink/beer/too strong

THE BEACH STORE

Rita is in the beach store right now. She wants to buy something. Listen!

Clerk: May I help you?
Rita: Yes, please. I am looking for a ***sun hat***.
Clerk: What color ***sun hat*** are you looking for?
Rita: I am looking for a ***yellow*** sun hat.
Clerk: Here is one.
Rita: Oh, great. How much is it?
Clerk: $7.99. Pay the cashier, please.

Now you go to the beach store.

This is what the store sells.

beach umbrella	$20.00
beach chair	$25.00
beach towel	$8.99
sun hat	$7.99
pair of sunglasses	$75.00
bottle of suntan lotion	$4.99
bottle of baby oil	$4.99
pair of sandals	$40.00

AN INVITATION TO A PARTY

<u>As you know,</u> Rose moved last month. She is inviting John to a party at her new place.

Rose: I want to invite you to a party at my new place.
John: Oh, great. I really want to see your new place. Did you buy a lot of new furniture?
Rose: Oh, yeah! I ***bought*** some new furniture three weeks ago. I'm waiting for a delivery right now.
John: ***Nice*** furniture is so expensive, you know.
Rose: Well, I ***shopped around*** and I found some ***bargains***. So anyway, I ***hope*** you can come to my party.
John: Sure. When is it?
Rose: It's on Friday, May 5th.
John: OK, Great!
Rose: And don't ***dress up*** for the party. It's casual.
John: Can I bring some ***booze***?
Rose: If you want to. But it's not necessary. My father ***bought*** a lot of food and liquor.
John: Your father is very ***generous***. Well, ***I have to go now***. I have to ***catch the bus***. See you on Friday.
Rose: See you then.

SUBSTITUTION DRILLS

I bought some new furniture.
chairs
tables
bookcases
pictures

I shopped around and I found some bargains.
sales
antiques
interesting things
good furniture

I hope you can come to my party.
wedding
birthday party
graduation
dinner party

Your father is very generous.
mother
boss
roommate
landlord

I have to go now. I have to catch the bus.
catch a plane
catch the train
get a taxi
go home

Fill in with the correct word.

SHOPPED AROUND, DELIVERY, DRESS UP, FURNITURE, BOOZE, CATCH A BUS, FRIDAY, HOPE, GENEROUS

1. Did you buy a lot of ___furniture___?
2. I'm waiting for a ___delivery___ right now.
3. I ___shopped___ ___around___ and I found some bargains.
4. I ___hope___ you can come to my party.
5. Don't ___dress___ ___up___ for the party. It's casual.
6. Can I bring some ___booze___?
7. Your father is very ___generous___.
8. Well, I have to go now. I have to ___catch a bus___.
9. See you on ___friday___.

QUESTIONS

1. What did Rose buy? Rose bought news furniture
2. What is Rose waiting for? she's waiting for a delivery
3. When is the party? The party it's on friday
4. Is it formal or casual? It is casual
5. Why does John have to go now? He has to catch the bus

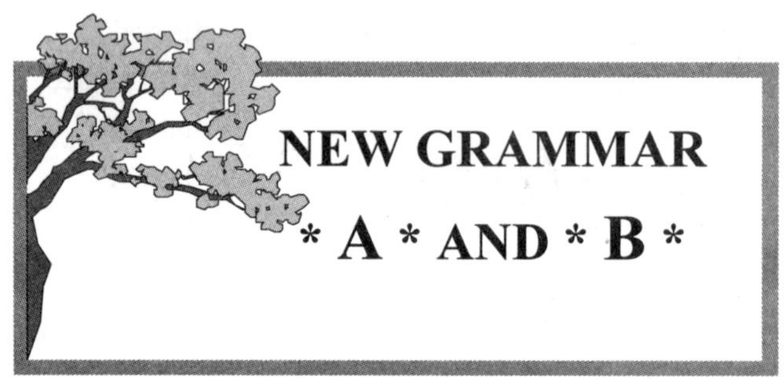

I BUY MY NEWSPAPER IN THE MORNING.
YESTERDAY, I BOUGHT MY NEWSPAPER IN THE AFTERNOON.

1 <u>Make a sentence in the past. Use one of the time expressions below.</u>

LAST WEEK/LAST MONTH/LAST YEAR/TWO YEARS AGO/A LONG TIME AGO/ YESTERDAY/THE OTHER DAY/A FEW MINUTES AGO

Example: **SWIM/SHE**
SHE SWAM LAST YEAR.

1. Buy a new home/they
   They bought a new home last year ✓
2. Eat in an ***outdoor*** cafe/John and Mary
   John and Mary ate in an outdoor yesterday ✓
3. Get up late/we
   We got up late a few minutes ago ✓
4. Leave NY/Alice
   Alice leaved NY a long time ago ✓
5. Come to my house/my classmates
   My classmates came to my house the other day ✓

6. Make ***chocolate cookies***/Judy

Judy maked chocolate cookies long time ago. (Made)

7. Run around the ***track***/I

I runed around the track the other day ✓

8. Sleep on the sofa/the ***guest***

The guest sleeped on the sofa yesterday ✓

9. Read an ***interesting*** story/I

I readed an interesting story lest week

10. Take out the garbage/we

We taked out the garbage a few minutes ago

11. Put on a brown jacket/I

I puted on a brown jacket the other day ✓

12. Go to the movies/the children

The children went to the movies last month ✓

2. <u>Change the sentence to the past.</u>

Example: I WORK IN AN OFFICE EVERY DAY.

I WORKED IN AN OFFICE <u>YESTERDAY.</u>

1. I smoke cigarettes every morning.

I smoked cigarettes yesterday ✓

2. We go to a party every night.

We went to a party in the last night ✓

3. We drink ***tea*** in the café on Saturday.

We drunk tea in the café on the last Saturday.

4. The new students study the book every afternoon.

The new studentes studied the book in the afternoon ✓

5. The young ***couple*** celebrate their wedding ***anniversary*** in June.

The young couple celebrated their wedding an. in the last June ✓

6. I put a little ***honey*** in my tea today.

I puted a little honey in my Tea yesterday ✓

7. The little boy brushes his teeth every night.

The little boy brushed his teeth lest night ✓

8. The ***gardener*** plants flowers every spring.
The gardener planted flowers in the last spring ✓

9. He takes out the ***garbage*** every morning.
He taked out the garbage last morning (took)

10. The officers shout at the soldiers in the afternoon.
The officers shouted at the soldiers in the last afternoon ✓

11. You get up late in the winter.
You geted up late in the last winter (got up)

12. Many Americans watch baseball games in the summer.
Many Americans watched baseball games ✓

13. I write a postcard at my desk.
I writed a postcast at my desk yesterday. (wrote)

14. You like the weather today.
You liked the weather yesterday ✓

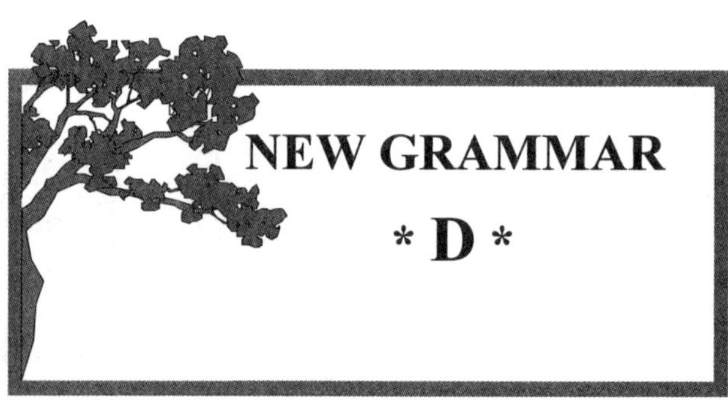

THESE HOUSES ARE FOR SALE.
THIS HOUSE IS FOR SALE.

1. <u>Change "these" to "this". Remember to change the verb when necessary.</u>

Example: **THESE DRESSES ARE LOVELY.**
THIS DRESS IS LOVELY.

1. These policemen are brave.
This policeman is brave ✓

2. These apartments are modern.
This apartment is modern ✓

3. These streets are narrow.
This street is narrow ✓

4. These cats sleep all day.
This cat sleeps all day. ✓

5. These children play in the park.
This child plays in the park. ✓

6. These farmers milk the cows.
This farmer milks the cows. ✓

7. These trucks deliver milk to the stores.
This truck ~~deliver~~ milk to the stores. (deliveres)

8. These fire engines make a lot of noise.
This fire enginier makes a lot of noise. ✓

9. These trains run express.
This train runs express. ✓

10. These bedrooms are messy.
This bedroom is messy ✓

THOSE TREES ARE UGLY.
THAT TREE IS BEAUTIFUL.

1. Change "those" to "that". Remember to change the verb when necessary.

Example: **THOSE BLOUSES ARE WASHABLE.**
THAT BLOUSE IS WASHABLE.

1. Those ***baby carriages*** are expensive.
That baby carriages is expensive ✓

2. Those ***boxes*** are empty.
That box is empty ✓

3. Those exercises are simple.
That exercise is simple ✓

4. Those tourists are having fun.
That tourist is having fun ✓

5. Those lawyers speak in ***court***.
That lawyer speaks in court ✓

6. Those motorcycles are fast.
That motorcycle is fast ✓

7. Those employees work hard.
That employee works hard. ✓

8. Those pills are strong.
That pill is strong. ✓

9. Those ***nurses*** help the doctor.
That nurse helps the doctor. ✓

10. Those managers are in a meeting.
That manager is in a meeting ✓

AN EVENING OUT IN NEW YORK

As you know, Yoshi visited Evelyn last year. One day, they went to the Statue of Liberty and two museums.

That evening, they had plans to ***eat out*** at a fancy restaurant. They made a reservation in advance. Yoshi ***liked*** the restaurant, but he didn't ***care for*** the food, so he didn't finish his meal. That night, they saw a Broadway musical. Yoshi enjoyed the music, but he only understood a little of the conversation. He got tired and ***fell asleep*** during the show. He snored a little, too.

Evelyn felt bad, but everyone knows you can't see New York in one week.

SUBSTITUTION DRILLS

They had plans to eat out at a fancy restaurant.
an expensive
a cheap
a Chinese
a small

He didn't ***care for*** the food.
wine
movie
music
school

He ***fell asleep*** during the show.
class
movie
meeting
concert

They had plans to eat out.
see a movie
go to a concert
take a walk
go sightseeing

As you know, Yoshi visited Evelyn last year.
two years ago
last week
the other day
yesterday

Fill in with the correct word.

MADE A RESERVATION, BROADWAY MUSICAL, UNDERSTOOD, SNORED, EAT OUT, CARE FOR, DIDN'T FINISH, FELL ASLEEP

1. They had plans to eat out at a fancy restaurant. ✓
2. They made a reservation in advance. ✓
3. Yoshi didn't care for the food. ✓
4. He didn't finish his meal. ✓
5. They saw a Broadway musical. ✓
6. He got tired and fell asleep. ✓
7. He snored a little, too. ✓
8. He understood only a little of the conversation. ✓

QUESTIONS

1. Where did they eat? They ate at a fancy restaurant.
2. Did Yoshi like the food? He didn't care for the food.
3. What did they see? They saw a Broadway musical
4. Did Yoshi understand the conversation? He understood a litte
5. What happened to Yoshi? He got tired and feel asleep and snored.
6. Did that ever happen to you?
   (If you say no, I don't believe you !!!)
7. Do you snore?
8. Did you watch TV last night? I didn't
9. Did you understand a little?
10. Did you understand your teacher yesterday?
    Yes, I understood the teacher yesterday

PROGRESSIVE SUBSTITUTION DRILLS

Change the sentence.

Example: HE DOESN'T SPEAK MUCH ENGLISH.

(I)

I DON'T SPEAK MUCH ENGLISH.

He doesn't speak much English.

Spanish I don't speak much Spanish ✓

understand I don't understand much Spanish ✓

we We don't understand much Spanish ✓

remember We don't remember much Spanish ✓

Chinese We don't remember much Chinese ✓

They sat down on the grass and had a picnic lunch.

snack They sat down on the grass and had a snack ✓
bench They sat down on the banch and had a snack ✓
she She sat down on the banch and had a snack ✓
beer She sat down on the banch and had a beer ✓
drank She sat down on the banch and drank a beer ✓

They waited for the boat.

subway They waited for the subway ✓
got on They got on ~~for~~ the subway ✓
got off They got off ~~for~~ the subway
she She got off ~~for~~ the subway
bus She got off ~~for~~ the bus

HOW TO STUDY ENGLISH

ALWAYS DO YOUR HOMEWORK <u>OUT LOUD</u>, EVEN IF IT IS WRITTEN HOMEWORK.

AT THE DOCTOR'S

As you know, Larry doesn't feel well today. He is at the doctor's office right now. The doctor is examining him.

Doctor: Lie down, Larry. Relax. Does it hurt here?
Larry: No, but my ***arms*** itch a lot.
Doctor: Well, don't ***scratch*** them. I think you have ***an allergy***. We have to take a few tests.
Sarah: Can you give us something for the itching right now?
Doctor: Yes, of course. Here is a ***prescription*** for a cream. It will stop the itching. And ***make an appointment*** with the nurse. Tell her it's for allergy ***tests***. Tell me, Larry, where did you go yesterday?
Larry: I went on a ***hike*** in the ***forest***.
Doctor: I see. What did you wear?
Larry: I wore shorts and a tee-shirt.
Doctor: So you didn't ***cover up*** your arms. Well, don't worry. You will feel better soon.

SUBSTITUTION DRILLS

My arms itch so much. Well, don't scratch them.
- legs
- hands
- shoulders
- elbows

What did you wear? I wore shorts.
- a bathing suit
- jeans
- boots
- a sweatshirt

Make an appointment with the nurse. Tell her it's for allergy tests.
x-rays
a check-up
blood tests
an examination

Fill in with the correct word.

~~ALLERGY~~, ~~SCRATCH~~, MAKE AN APPOINTMENT, ~~HIKE~~, ~~PRESCRIPTION~~, ~~COVER UP~~, ~~WORE~~

1. I went on a hike in the forest. ✓
2. My arms itch so much.
   Well, don't scratch them. ✓
3. I think you have an allergy. ✓
4. Here is a prescription for a cream. ✓
5. So you didn't cover up your arms and legs. ✓
6. Make an appointment with the nurse. ✓
7. I wore shorts and a tee-shirt. ✓

QUESTIONS

1. Where did Larry go yesterday? He went on a hike in the forest
2. What did he wear? He wore shorts and a tee-shirt
3. Did he cover up his arms and legs? No, he didn't
4. Did you ever have an allergy? No, I ~~didn't~~ have an allergy.
   No, I never have an allergy.

Perguntas em:
did, does, is, do
Respostas no negativo:
didn't, doesn't, isn't, don't

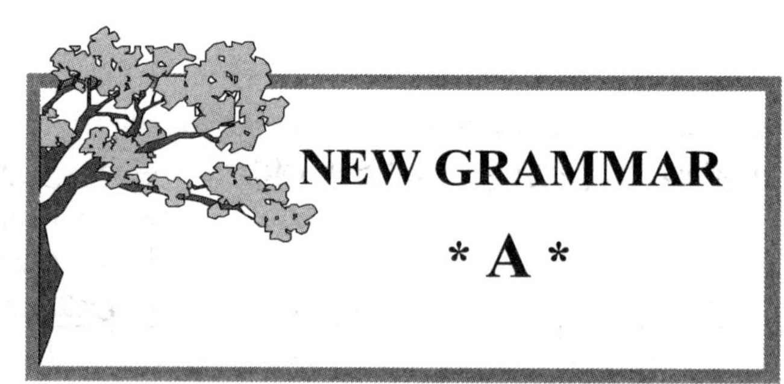

WHERE DO YOU WORK?
WHERE DID YOU WORK LAST MONTH?

1. **Change to a question with "did". Use one of the following past time expressions.**

in 1985/last summer/last winter/last spring

last fall/a year ago/before today's class/a long time ago

Example: **WHERE DO YOU EAT YOUR LUNCH?**

WHERE DID YOU EAT YOUR LUNCH YESTERDAY?

1. Does Theresa live on a farm?
   Did Theresa live on a farm a long time ago? ✓
2. When does your husband come home from work?
   When did your husband come home from work before today's class? ✓
3. Do you drive a car?
   Did you drive a car the last summer? ✓
4. Does your father drive on ***the highway***?
   Did your father drive on the highway before today's class? ✓
5. Does the bus stop at the stop sign?
   Did the bus stop at the stop sign last fall? ✓
6. When does the driver ***blow the horn***?
   When did the driver blow the horn a long time ago? ✓
7. Do you get gas for your car every day?
   Did you get gas for your car every day in 1985?
8. Does your car need a ***tune-up***?
   Did you car need a tune-up a long time ago? ✓

9. Do you take the bus every day?

Did you take the bus every day in the last summer?

10. Do you forget your medicine?

Did you forget your medicine before today's class?

11. When do you ***slice*** the vegetables?

When did you slice the vegetables in the last winter?

12. Do you go ***skydiving***?

Did you go skydiving a long time ago? ✓

WHEN DID YOU PLAY TENNIS?

I PLAYED TENNIS LAST WEEK.

1. <u>Ask a question and answer it.</u>

Example: **OPEN THE STORE/WHAT TIME? (YOU) (7:30)**

WHAT TIME DID YOU OPEN THE STORE?
I OPENED THE STORE AT 7:30.

1. Listen to heavy metal music/where/they (at the club)

did they

Where ~~they did~~ listen to h.m. music ?

They listened at the club .

2. Paint the apartment/when?/they (yesterday)

did they

When ~~they did~~ paint the apartment?

They painted the apartment yesterday

3. Put the empty glasses/where?/you (in the sink)
Where did you put the empty glasses?
I put the empty glasses in the sink. ✓

4. Wash his jacket/when?/he (two days ago)
When ~~he did~~ did he wash his jacket?
He washed his jacket two days ago.

5. Speak with/who?/Kathy (her friend)
Who ~~Kathy did~~ did Kathy speak with?
Kathy spoke with her friend.

6. Write that long letter to/who?/he (his father-in-law)
Who ~~he did~~ did he write that long letter to?
He wrote it to his father-in-law.

7. Answer the door/when?/you (a few minutes ago)
When did you answer the door? ✓
I answered a few minute ago. ✓

8. Get a perm/where?/your sister (at the beauty salon)
Where did your sister get a perm? ✓
She got up at the beauty salon. ✓

9. Deliver the package/when?/they (a little while ago)
When ~~they did~~ did they deliver the package? ✓
They delivered a little while ago.

10. See the super/where?/you (downstairs)
Where did you see the super?
I saw the super downstairs. ✓

11. Put in the soup/what?/the cooks (a lot of salt)
What did the cooks put in the soup? ✓
They put a lot of salt in the soup.

12. Walk through the park with /who?/you (my boyfriend)
Who did you walk through the park? with
I walked with my boyfriend. ✓

2. Answer the following questions. Be careful, some questions are with "do" or "does" and some with "did".

Example: **WHEN DID YOU COME TO THIS COUNTRY?**
I CAME TO THIS COUNTRY LAST YEAR.

WHERE DO YOU BUY FOOD?
I BUY FOOD IN THE SUPERMARKET.

1. What time do you get up every day?
I get up at 8am every day

2. When does the teacher come into the classroom?
He comes to the classroom at 4 o'clock

3. Where did your husband go yesterday?
He went to the market yesterday

4. What do you usually eat for breakfast?
I usually ate a bread for breakfast

5. What time did you get home last night?
I got home last night at 7 o'clock

6. Where does your mother live?
She lives in Brazil

7. Where does your father work?
He works

8. Who did the teacher speak with before the class?
He spoke with his friends before the class.

9. Who did you see yesterday?
I saw my classmates yesterday

10. What time does the laundromat close?
The laundromat closed at 10 pm.

11. When do you usually visit your relatives?
I usually visit my relatives once a week.

12. When did you visit your relatives last year?
I visited my relatives last year in the summer.

13. What time did you take a shower yesterday?
I took a shower at 2 o'clock ✓

14. When did you have a ***snack*** last night?
I didn't have a snack last night ✓

15. When did you begin this class?
I began this class two weeks ago ✓

HERMAN AND MYRTLE - Part II

Myrtle: Hi, honey. I'm home.
Herman: Hi. Did you have a nice day?
Myrtle: Oh, ok. Herman, did you talk to your boss today?
Herman: Yes, ***I talked to my boss today***.
Myrtle: Did you ask for a raise?
Herman: Yes, I asked for a raise.

Now you continue.

Myrtle: Did you call to your mother?
Herman: Yes, I called to her.

HERE ARE SOME PHRASES

buy new tires
play golf with the guys
have a drink with your client
fix the roof
mow the lawn
change the light bulbs
hang the curtains
carry the packages upstairs
clean the attic
wash the car
help the children with their homework
move the bed
get some car insurance
buy a personal computer

3. <u>Ask a question. Be careful! Sometimes you must use "do" or "does" and sometimes "did".</u>

Example: **THEY WATCHED TV LAST NIGHT.** **(WHAT TIME)?**
WHAT TIME DID THEY WATCH TV LAST NIGHT?

THEY WATCH TV. **(WHAT TIME)?**
WHAT TIME DO THEY WATCH TV?

THEY LIKE THE NEWS REPORT ON CHANNEL 4. **(YOU ALSO)?**

DO YOU____
DO YOU LIKE THE NEWS REPORT ON CHANNEL 4, ALSO?

HE READS A NEWSPAPER IN THE MORNING. **(WHAT NEWSPAPER)?**
WHAT NEWSPAPER DOES HE READ IN THE MORNING?

1. We played soccer last week/where?
Where did they play soccer last week?

2. We play soccer every week/where?
where do we play soccer every week?

3. We took a vacation last year. (they-also)
They did take a vacation last year, also?

4. We take a vacation every year. (they-also)
They do take a vacation every year, also?

5. They ate pizza last weekend. (spaghetti)
They did eat spaghetti last weekend?

6. They eat pizza every weekend. (spaghetti-too)
They do eat pizza every weekend too?

7. You came to America/when?
When do you came to America?

8. You come to America every year. (why)
Why do you come to America every year?

9. He spoke with his mother last night. (his fiancée-too)
____?

10. He speaks with his mother every night. (his fiancée-too)
____?

11. She translated a letter. (when)
When does she translate a letter?

12. She translates letters. (when)
When does She translate letters?

13. They buy new shoes every year. (why)
why did they buy new shoes every year?

14. You came to work yesterday. (how)
How do you come to work yesterday?

15. He turns on the TV every evening. (what time)
What time does he turn on the TV every evening?

16. Alice wanted to leave N.Y. (why)
Why does Alice want to leave N.Y.?

17. The nurse took his temperature. (when)
When does the nurse take his temperature?

18. You usually pay your bills. (when)
When do you usually pay your bills?

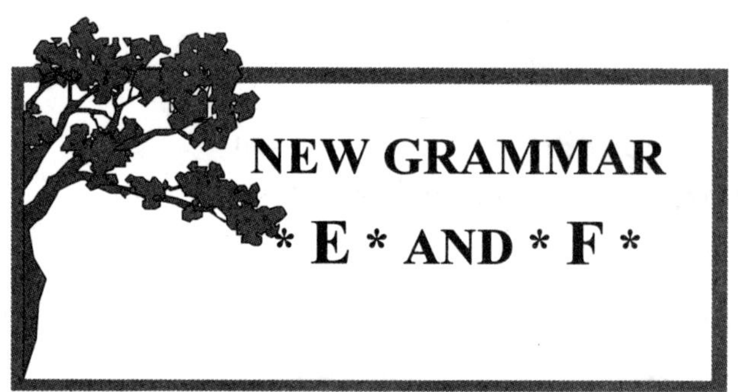

THE WASTEBASKET IS UNDER THE TABLE.
BOB IS SITTING BETWEEN HELEN AND LARRY.

1. Answer the questions.

1. Where is the can of paint? (under the ladder)

____

2. Where is the picture? (behind the desk)

____

3. Where is the TV? (under the VCR)

____

4. Where are the people? (in front of the library)

____

5. Where are the man and woman? (behind the street light)

____

6. Where is the teacher? (next to the two students)

____

7. Where is the ***ambulance***? (in front of the hospital)

____

DRAW A PICTURE

One student will read this story. Another student will draw a picture.

I

This is my bedroom. My bed is in front of the window. My ***night table*** is next to my bed. My dresser is on ***the other side*** of the room, across from my bed. My dresser is ***between*** the door and the closet. A picture is behind the dresser.

II

This is my kitchen. The sink is ***between*** the refrigerator and the stove. The refrigerator is ***on the right*** and the stove is ***on the left***. The table is in the middle of the room. The table ***is under*** a big light. A ***calendar*** is on the wall ***behind*** the table.

III

This is my office. My desk is in the middle of the room. The ***waste basket*** is under the desk. The telephone is on the desk, on the left. The dictionary is next to the telephone. A chair is in front of the desk.

IV

This is my favorite restaurant. There is a big counter. Two waitresses are ***behind*** the counter. Some ***stools*** are ***in front of*** the counter. The napkins are on the counter. The ***ketchup*** is next to the napkins.

V

This is my favorite supermarket.

The fruits and vegetables are in aisle 1. The oranges are next to the apples. The frozen food is in aisle 4. The ***frozen vegetables*** are between the cake and the ***TV dinners***. The ***checkout counter*** is near the door. The ***cashier*** is behind the counter.

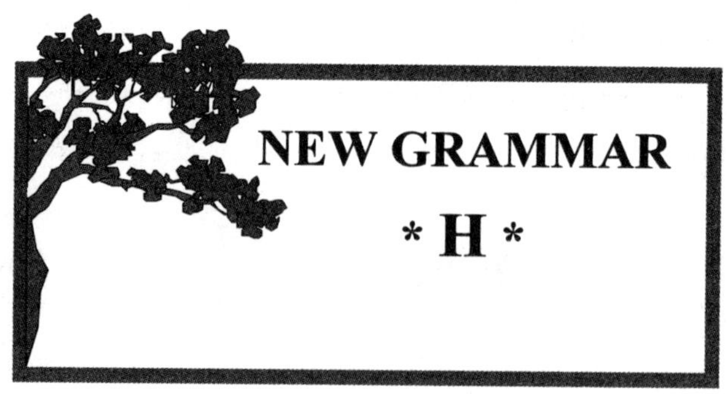

DID YOU PLAY GOLF LAST SUNDAY?
NO, I DIDN'T PLAY GOLF LAST SUNDAY.

1. **Change to a sentence with "didn't.**

Example: **I CALLED UP PETER LAST NIGHT.** **(ROBERT)**

I DIDN'T CALL UP ROBERT LAST NIGHT.

1. I played the piano yesterday. (the guitar)

____

2. She ***sang*** a country song last week. (a rock song)

____

3. Mrs. Smith ***wore*** high heels to work. (sneakers)

____

4. I sat close to the door. (the radiator)

____

5. I washed the cups and ***saucers***. (pots and pans)

____

6. The cat ***slept*** on the floor. (on the sofa)

____

7. The baby ***coughed*** all night. (all day)

____

8. The waiters served the drinks quickly. (the food)

____

9. They had a lot of fun on Saturday. (on Wednesday)

____

10. We understood your question. (answer)

____

2. **Use the correct form of the verb.**

Example: I STARTED A NEW JOB YESTERDAY.

START/STARTED

MY MOTHER

My mother ***loves/loved*** to stay home every night. She usually ***cooks/cooked*** a nice dinner and then she ***watches/watched*** TV. She never ***goes/went*** out. So last night I ***try/tried*** to call her on the telephone. I ***hear/heard*** the telephone ring many times, but my mother didn't ***pick/picked*** up the phone. So I ***call/called*** my aunt. I said, "My mother is not home. Where did she ***go/went***?" My aunt said, "She ***go/went*** to the hospital." I asked, "When did she ***go/went*** there?" My aunt said, "She ***leave/left*** the house a few hours ago." I said, "Why did she ***need/needed*** to go to the hospital?" My aunt said, "Don't worry. She always ***visits/visited*** her friend on Thursday evening. But she usually ***come/comes*** home early."

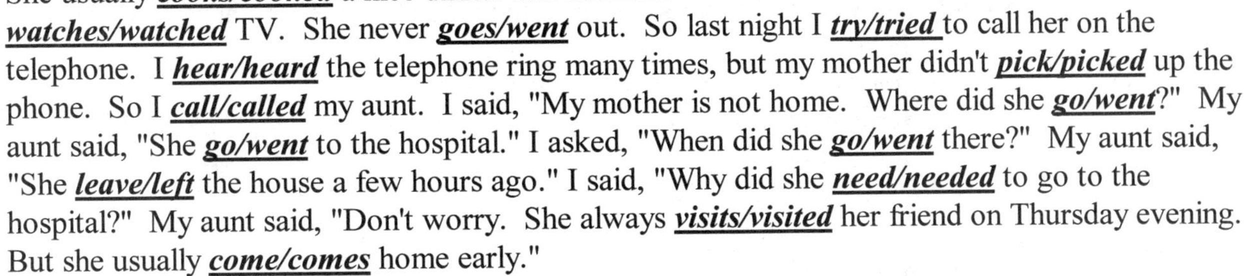

After that conversation, I ***decide/decided*** to go to the movies. I called the theater and I asked, "What time does the movie ***start/started***?" The man answered, "You are late. The movie ***begin/began*** a half hour ago." I was sad. I always ***speak/spoke*** to my mother in the evening, but I didn't ***speak/spoke*** to her last night. And I always ***see/saw*** a movie in the evening, but I didn't ***see/saw*** a movie last night. ***Better luck next time***.

AN UNPLEASANT EVENING

As you know, John and Mary didn't go dancing last night.

Robert: What did you and Mary do last night?

John: We went to the movies. But I think Mary is ***mad*** at me.

Robert Did you two have an ***argument***?

John: No, we didn't have an argument, but we didn't have a good time, either.

Robert: What do you mean?

John: Well, Mary usually enjoys movies, but she didn't enjoy the movie last night. And she usually drinks beer, but she didn't drink beer last night. She drank diet soda instead.

Robert: Uh, huh!

John: And she didn't want to have a snack after the movie. She didn't smile very much. She ***frowned*** a lot and she looked upset. And when we got back to her place, she didn't invite me in. I am concerned about her.

Robert: What's the matter with Mary?

John: Well, she wants to get married, but I don't want to get married yet.

Robert: I see. It sounds like you and Mary need to have a ***serious discussion***.

John: I guess so. See you later.

SUBSTITUTION DRILLS

Mary is mad at me.
him
her
us
them

Mary usually enjoys movies, but she didn't enjoy the movie last night.
likes
goes to
remembers
understands

She drank diet soda instead.
orange juice
water
coffee
wine

She frowned a lot and she looked upset.
sad
nervous
angry
unhappy

My parents got married very young.
friends
older sister
neighbors
classmate
teacher

Fill in with the correct word.

DIET SODA, CONCERNED, MAD AT ME,
ARGUMENT, SERIOUS DISCUSSION, SNACK, FROWNED

1. I think Mary is ____________ ____________ ____________.
2. Did you two have an ______________________________?
3. She didn't drink beer last night. She drank ____________ ____________ instead.
4. She didn't want to have a ____________ after the movie.
5. She ____________ a lot and she looked upset.
6. I am ____________ about her.
7. You two need to have a ____________ ____________.

QUESTIONS

1. Where did John and Mary go last night?
2. Did Mary have a good time?
3. Did she enjoy the movie?
4. Did she drink beer?
5 What did she drink?
6. Did Mary want a snack after the movie?
7. How does John feel about Mary?
8. What's the matter with Mary?
9. Why doesn't John want to get married?
10. Do you want to get married?

SUSAN'S GRANDMOTHER

Susan is very ***concerned*** about her grandmother. Susan's grandmother is very old. She is not sick right now, but she is not very healthy, ***either***. She is weak.

Last month, she had a bad ***accident*** in the house. There were some flowers on the ***window sill***. One day, grandmother was alone in the house. She wanted to change the water in the vase. When she ***reached*** over, she ***lost her balance*** and she fell. Susan took her grandmother to the hospital. The doctor examined her and she took x-rays. Susan's grandmother ***sprained***uher back, but she was all right. She is resting at home right now.

SUBSTITUTION DRILLS

Susan is concerned about her grandmother.
aunt
mother
brother
father-in-law

Last month, she had a bad accident in the house.
in the car
in the supermarket
on the way home
in front of the house

Susan took her grandmother to the hospital.
doctor
dentist
lawyer
eye-doctor

The doctor took some x-rays.
looked at
wanted
studied
needed

Fill in with the correct word.

EXAMINED, CONCERNED ABOUT, X-RAYS, ALL RIGHT, HEALTHY, ACCIDENT, WINDOW SILL, LOST HER BALANCE, SPRAINED

1. Susan is very _______________ _______________ her grandmother.
2. She is not sick right now, but she is not _______________ either.
3. There were some flowers on the _______________ _______________.
4. When she reached over, she _______________ _______________ _______________.
5. The doctor _______________ her.
6. The doctor took some _______________.
7. Susan's grandmother _______________ her back.
8. She was _______________ _______________.
9. She had a bad _______________ in the house.

QUESTIONS

1. How is Susan's grandmother?
2. What was on the window sill?
3. What happened when Susan's grandmother reached over?
4. Where did Susan take her grandmother?
5. What did the doctor do?

6. How is Susan's grandmother now?
7. What is she doing right now?
8. Did you ever have an accident? What happened?
9. Do you have flowers at home?
10. Do you change the water every day?

REVIEW

WRITE

Invite a friend in the class to go out Saturday night. Copy and complete a letter to your friend.

Example: **Hi, Alice:**

1. Let's get together this ***Saturday night***.
2. We can go to a ***rock club***.
3. There is a good rock club ***on Bleecker Street***.
4. We can ***listen to the music and drink beer*** and talk.
5. We can get there at ***10:00***.
6. Call me if you want to go.

See You Later,

Bob

1. Answer the question.

Example: **WHERE DID YOU GO YESTERDAY?** **(TO THE STORE)**
I WENT TO THE STORE.

1. What time did you get up? (at 8:00 AM)

____

2. When did you see your boss? (yesterday)

____

3. What did he do last night? (his homework)

____

4. Who did you see last month? (my friend)

____

5. Where did she eat lunch? (in the café)

____

6. Where did you buy that bag? (uptown)

____

7. When did you come to New York? (2 years ago)

____

8. What time did they leave school? (at 1:00 PM)

____

9. Where did you meet your friend? (at school)

____

10. What time did the students begin class? (at 10:00 AM)

____

2. <u>Answer the following questions. Be careful. Some questions are with "do" or "does" and some with "did".</u>

Example: **WHEN DID YOU COME TO THIS COUNTRY?**
I CAME TO THIS COUNTRY LAST YEAR.

WHERE DO YOU BUY FOOD?
I BUY FOOD IN THE SUPERMARKET.

1. What time do you go to bed every night?

____

2. What time do you take a break?

____

3. Where did you go after class yesterday?

____

4. What do you usually eat for breakfast?

____

5. What time did you come to school today?

____

6. Where does your best friend live?

____

7. Where did you work last year?

____

8. What time does the supermarket close?

____

9. What time did you brush your teeth yesterday?

____

10 When did you have a ***snack*** last night?

____

11. When did you begin this class?

____

3. **Change the question and answer the new question.**

A: DID YOU BUY THAT MAGAZINE?
B: YES, I BOUGHT THAT MAGAZINE.

book?
newspaper?
dictionary?
notebook?
pad?
map?

A: DID YOU BUY THAT MAGAZINE?
B: YES, I BOUGHT THAT MAGAZINE.

read
look at
pick up
like
enjoy

A: DID YOU BUY THAT MAGAZINE?
B: YES, I BOUGHT THAT MAGAZINE.
read/newspaper
use/dictionary
write in/notebook
pay for/class
enjoy/textbook
understand/subway map
study/driver's manual
borrow/pen
put away/address book

A: DID YOU BUY THAT MAGAZINE?
B: YES, I BOUGHT THAT MAGAZINE.

read/this newspaper
enjoy/these books
like/that/textbook
pay for school

4. **Answer the following questions. Be careful. Some questions are with "do" or "does" and some are with "did".**

Example: **DID YOU SHAVE YESTERDAY?**
YES, I SHAVED YESTERDAY.

DO YOU WATCH TV EVERY NIGHT?
YES, I WATCH TV EVERY NIGHT.

1. Did he buy flowers for his wife?

____

2. Does he always ***celebrate*** his birthday?

____

3. Does he take a ***coffee break*** in the morning?

____

4. Did you study ***carefully*** last night?

____

5. Did you ***scrub*** that pot completely?

____

6. Does she mop the floor every day?

____

7. Did you see the ***stop sign***?

____

8. Do the children enjoy ***snow***?

____

9. Does the fine engine make a lot of noise?

____

10. Did the sanitation workers ***pick up*** the garbage last Thursday?

____

11. Did the police catch the thief?

____

12. Do you sometimes wear ***sandals***?

____

5. Answer the question with "us" or "them".

Example: **DID YOU WANT TO SEE ME?** **(THEM)**
NO, I WANTED TO SEE THEM.

1. Did John visit her? (us)

____

2. Did the teacher help you? (them)

____

3. Did he speak to you? (them)

____

4. Did Allan buy flowers for his girlfriend? (us)

____

5. Does Kathy live close to him? (us)

____

6. Does that mechanic work for you? (them)

____

7. Do you often travel with her? (them)

____

8. Is that pasta for him? (us)

____

9. Did you take a picture of me? (them)

____

10. Did she play tennis with him? (us)

____

6. Make a sentence with "didn't".

Example: **WRITE HER A LETTER/I**
I DIDN'T WRITE HER A LETTER.

1. Ride a motorcycle. (I)

____

2. Explain the story. (I)

____

3. Take the baby's temperature. (the nurse)

____

4. Go on vacation. (the students)

____

5. Have a dishwasher. (my grandmother)

____

6. Build a big house. (the men)

____

7. See the accident. (the children)

____

8. Know this address. (I)

____

9. Accept the check. (the store)

____

10. Delivery the package. (the mailman)

____

PROGRESSIVE SUBSTITUTION DRILLS

1. They saw a late movie last night.

he ______________________________

early ______________________________

show ______________________________

last week ______________________________

watch ______________________________

2. Did he travel to another city?

they ______________________________

country ______________________________

go ______________________________

the tourists______________________________

town ______________________________

3. Susan made a beautiful dress last week.

skirt ______________________________

the woman______________________________

bought ______________________________

wore ______________________________

month ______________________________